SCRIPTURE HEALING

How to ~~Play~~ *Pray Scripture*
Play with these ideas…

PUBLISHER:
Kenneth L. Fabbi, Lethbridge, Alberta, Canada

Email: FiveFoldCycle@gmail.com

Copyright © 2019 by Kenneth L. Fabbi
All rights reserved.

Scripture taken from New Revised Standard Version (NRSV), New Revised Standard Version Bible, copyright © 1989 the Division of Christian Education of the National Council of the Churches of Christ in the United States of America. Used by permission. All rights reserved.

No part of this publication may be reproduced in any form, or by any means, electronic or mechanical, including photocopying, recording, or any information browsing, storage, or retrieval system, without permission in writing from the Author.

Kenneth would welcome your communication at FiveFoldCycle@gmail.com.

ISBN:
Paperback: 978-0-9952039-5-2
eBook: 978-0-9952039-6-9

SUBJECTS: *Scripture - - Healing Prayer - - Christianity - - Meditation - - Scriptural Healing - - Growth*

I. Title   II. Fabbi, Kenneth L.

SCRIPTURE HEALING

How to ~~Play~~ Pray Scripture
Play with these ideas...

INDEX:

ACKNOWLEDGEMENTS 4

INTRODUCTION 5

LET'S NOW LOOK AT SCRIPTURE AS PRAYER 6

SECTION ONE: *MAKING SCRIPTURE A PERSONAL PRAYER* 8

NOTE FROM THE AUTHOR: There is a hole only God Can Fill 16

SECTION TWO: *PROCLAMATION – PROCLAIMING GOD'S WORD* 17

SECTION THREE: *SEEKING HIS PROMISES* 34

SECTION FOUR: *PUTTING YOURSELF IN THE STORY* 42

NOTES 62

APPENDIX 1: WHAT IS PRAYER 63

ACKNOWLEDGEMENTS:

As this booklet was coming to completion, I asked a few people to look it over with those critical proof-reading editor's eyes. It is always amazing to see what they see and receive their input.

A big thank you to Sandy Whyte who offered many important insights. I appreciate you Sandy.

My cousin Dianne Palmer, I appreciate your review, because it catches me in some un-spoken assumptions and my 'Christianese' language. Thank you for making things clearer!

Karla Conte, I would like to thank you very, very much for taking the time to review and edit the manuscript. It is that love and prayerful care that makes these projects a blessing to all that read them. Thank you.

INTRODUCTION:

> God's Mercy never ends!!!
> Lamentations 3:22-23

We know that Scripture Heals & God's Mercy never ends!

This booklet is meant to walk you through a collection of Scriptures from the Holy Bible. Each Scripture offers a truth. Many of the Scriptural passages offer insight into healing and God's design.

This booklet will help you use Scripture to pray. It is meant to expand the way you pray Scripture. It will expose you to 4 different methods of praying Scripture.

I encourage you to play and experiment with these ideas and share them with your friends. *I encourage you to ~~play~~ pray with these ideas!*

As you may know, I already have some material published on healing prayer entitled *Five Fold Cycle - Method of Healing Personal Hurt*[1], which includes a section *'Scripture As Medicine'*. You might take a look at that material, as another resource, to understand how and why God uses Scripture to heal our mind, memories, emotions and the like – we call this Inner Healing.

LET'S NOW LOOK AT SCRIPTURE AS PRAYER:

> How to make scripture count!

In this work, I will offer some insights into how to use scripture, how to apply it and how to receive the fruit available.

> [22] *By contrast, the fruit of the Spirit is love, joy, peace, patience, kindness, generosity, faithfulness,* [23] *gentleness, and self-control. There is no law against such things.*
> **Galatians 5:22-23**

Who does God heal: how does God heal? In wandering through the Bible, we see that time after time Jesus healed those with little faith and those with little or no understanding of things of God.

We also see that God wants to walk with us and we with Him. The image you might remember as you go through this material is that of Adam and Eve in the garden before the fall. God walked with them. He is your God.

I am Your God

In this booklet there are a number of sections, each offering an alternate way to use and approach scripture for healing. They include:

- **Making Scripture A Personal Prayer**
- **Proclamation**
    – Proclaiming God's Word
- **Seeking His Promises**
- **Putting Yourself In The Story**

Enjoy this scriptural journey!

SECTION ONE:

MAKING SCRIPTURE A PERSONAL PRAYER.

We begin by realizing that there are some conditions that you and I must follow to access the Lord's healing. Yes, He does heal those who have little knowledge of Him and little or no faith, but healing is assured if we meet some conditions.

> Healing belongs to His children!

The conditons are simple: placing Him first and follow His Voice.

In Section One we will put each Scripture into a personal prayer. In this manner we become interactive and personal with our God and He with us.

> There is always a clear direction in Scripture that we hear and follow God's Voice!

Exodus 15:26 – If you follow my voice, I will not bring any of the diseases against you for I am the Lord who heals.

> *²⁶ He said, "If you will listen carefully to the voice of the LORD your God, and do what is right in his sight, and give heed to his commandments and keep all his statutes, I will not bring upon you any of the diseases that I brought upon the Egyptians; for I am the LORD who heals you."*
>
> *I am the God who heals*

> We make this personal...
> Put your name in the space.

Let's Pray: Lord, I _____ will follow Your Commands and listen carefully to Your voice. Lead me, teach me and I will keep Your statutes. In doing these things, I will not receive from You, diseases of old, for You are the Lord who heals me.

> Promise of blessing for obedience.
> Making God 1st in our lives.

Exodus 23:25-26 – Worship the Lord your God, and He will bless you and take away sickness from among you.

> *25 You shall worship the LORD your God, and I will bless your bread and your water; and I will take sickness away from among you. 26 No one shall miscarry or be barren in your land; I will fulfill the number of your days.*

Let's Pray: Lord I _____ worship You, You are my God. You promise and assure me that You will bless my bread and water and take sickness away from me, my family and my people. You promise as well, that there will be no miscarrying or barrenness in my land and that we will fulfill the number of our days.

WITH OUR PROMISE OF OBEDIENCE WE ARE ASSURED THAT WE WILL RECEIVE HIS BLESSING!

> We have confidence because God is fighting for us!

Deuteronomy 3:22 – Moses is charging Joshua and says 'Do not fear God fights for you.

> *²² "Do not fear them, for it is the Lord your God who fights for you."*

> We make this personal… Put your name in the space.

Let's Pray: Lord I _____ will not fear, for You my God fight for me!

WE HAVE CONFIDENCE BECAUSE OUR GOD IS THE CREATOR KNOWN AS THE GREAT I AM!

> Once again, we have confidence and are assured of God's blessing for obedience!

Deuteronomy 7:14-15 – You will be most blessed and the Lord will turn away every illness.

> *¹⁴ You shall be the most blessed of peoples, with neither sterility nor barrenness among you or your livestock. ¹⁵ The LORD will turn away from you every illness; all the dread diseases of Egypt that you experienced, he will not inflict on you, but he will lay them on all who hate you.*

Let's Pray: Lord, I _____ believe that in You I will be most blessed, as will my possessions. I _____ believe that You will turn away every illness and disease from me.

WE TAKE OUR POSITION AS CHILDREN OF OUR GREAT GOD AND APPROPRIATE THE BLESSING AVAILABLE TO US!

> As children of God we are made right before God through Jesus's suffering.

1 Peter 2:24 – He bore our sins and by His wounds we are healed.

> *²⁴ He himself bore our sins in his body on the cross, so that, free from sins, we might live for righteousness; by his wounds (stripes) you have been healed.*

Let's Pray: Father, I _____ believe, that through Your Son's death on the Cross and resurrection my sins are removed and I am righteous before You. I _____ also accept that by Jesus' stripes I am made whole in body, in mind and in soul.

> We, as children of our God, have confidence in asking of Him.

1 John 5:14-15 – In boldness we come before Him and ask.

> *¹⁴ And this is the boldness we have in him, that if we ask anything according to his will, he hears us. ¹⁵ And if we know that he hears us in whatever we ask, we know that we have obtained the requests made of him.*

Let's Pray: Father, I _____ come before You as Your child and ask for _____ . I know that You hear me and that whatever I ask according to Your will, it will be obtained.

> We are invited to abide in Him.

John 15:7 – When you abide in Me ask and it will be done.

> ⁷ *If you abide in me, and my words abide in you, ask for whatever you wish, and it will be done for you.*

Let's Pray: Lord, I _____ abide in You and Your Words are welcome to abide in me. I _____ ask You Lord _____, knowing that You hear me.

> Blessed are those who have not seen but believe.

John 20:29 – Although we have not seen Jesus, we are blessed because we believe.

> ²⁹ *Jesus said to him, "Have you believed because you have seen me? Blessed are those who have not seen and yet have come to believe."*

Let's Pray: Lord, I _____ believe in You. Your Words say, I _____ am blessed if I have not seen but believe.

NOTE FROM THE AUTHOR:

THERE IS A HOLE

ONLY GOD CAN FILL

You will note by now that there is an underlying assumption in the Scripture. It can be defined by two words 'Our Relationship'.

We are created beings, each of us unique and individual. Each of us has his or her own finger print, his or her own iris biometric and his or her own DNA. No one will carry this uniqueness. No one will be like you.

We were created by the Master Craftsman, God the Father in Heaven. God gave us life and looks to share that life with us. It is said that in each of us is a *God Size Hole*, that only He can fill. That hole is 'Our Relationship'.

We necessarily need to turn to God, the Designer, who created us. This implies opening and joining with Him in this creative movement – our life.

As we join with Him, open to His Holy Spirit [2] in our life, we will feel His peace and satisfaction in our life.

> If you reverence the Lord
> you will lack no good thing.
> Psalm 34:10-11

In this relationship, we can take our position as Children of our great God and appropriate the blessings available to us!

SECTION TWO:

PROCLAMATION –

PROCLAIMING GOD'S WORD

In Section Two we are going to add a new method of praying Scripture called Proclamation. You are invited to proclaim the Scripture over your lives, your situation and over the world around you.

The idea is simple, we take the position that our great God has made us His adoptive children and in that relationship we gain the ability to appropriate the blessings available. These blessings were already paid for and given to us by Jesus' death on the Cross and

His resurrection. One could say and logically conclude that these things are already done. We simply have to step into them.

> Blessings overcome us when we stand on His truth!

Deuteronomy 28:1-2 – Blessings for obedience, will overtake us.

> *¹If you will only obey the LORD your God, by diligently observing all his commandments that I am commanding you today, the LORD your God will set you high above all the nations of the earth; ² all these blessings shall come upon you and overtake you, if you obey the LORD your God:*

Proclamation: Lord, I _____ will obey and observe Your Commandments. And I trust in Your Word that all the blessings will come on me and overtake me.

A Proclamation is an act of declaring or decreeing a Scriptural fact.

In speaking the Proclamation we are joining with God in His Word and His Authority.

We speak God's Word as a covering over a situation for example our family.

We know that God's Word when spoken will be accomplished.
Isaiah 55: 11

> There was an Exchange on the Cross . . .

Isaiah 53:4-5 – Surely He took our infirmities – by His wounds we are Healed.

> *⁴ Surely he has borne our infirmities and carried our diseases; yet we accounted him stricken, struck down by God, and afflicted. ⁵ But he was wounded for our transgressions, crushed for our iniquities; upon him was the punishment that made us whole, and by his bruises we are healed.*

Proclamation: Lord I _____ believe that there was an exchange on the Cross and that You took my infirmities and diseases; You were afflicted and struck down by my transgressions and crushed by my iniquity. I _____ proclaim that You took on the punishment and through You I _____ am made whole. Further I _____ proclaim that by Your bruises I am healed.

Now try praying this scripture by proclaiming it over your family, your situation or the community around you.

Proclamation for Families: Lord I _____ believe that there was an exchange on the Cross and that You took my families infirmities and diseases; You were afflicted and struck down by their transgressions and crushed by their iniquity. I _____ proclaim that You took on the punishment and through You (they) _____ are made whole. Further I _____ proclaim that by Your bruises they are healed.

> **IN PROCLAMATION, WE STAND ON THE ROCK, JESUS, AND IN HIM AND THROUGH THE FATHER WE PROCLAIM A TRUTH FROM SCRIPTURE!**

> Make this Scripture your prayer and proclamation . . .

Jeremiah 17:14 – Heal me oh Lord and I will be healed.

> ¹⁴ *Heal me, O LORD, and I shall be healed; save me, and I shall be saved; for you are my praise.*

A Prayer of Proclamation: Lord, I _____ proclaim that You are my God! Heal me, O Lord, and I shall be healed; save me, and I shall be saved; for You are my praise.

AS WE LEARN AND INTERIORIZE SCRIPTURE, WE ARE MORE ABLE TO STAND STRONG IN THE FACE OF CONFLICT !

> Our Rights and Protection under Jesus include: light, salvation, no fear & safety in His strong hold.

Psalm 27:1 – The Lord is my light, my salvation and my strong hold, whom shall I fear?

¹ The LORD is my light and my salvation; whom shall I fear? The LORD is the stronghold of my life; of whom shall I be afraid?

A Prayer of Proclamation & Confidence: Lord, I _____ have confidence and I _____ proclaim, that You are my Light and my Salvation, therefore I will not fear. Lord, You are the stronghold of my life and I will not be afraid!

Now try praying this scripture by proclaiming it over your family, your situation or the community around you.

A Prayer of Proclamation & Confidence for our family or situation: Lord, I _____ have confidence and proclaim, that You are the Light and the Salvation for _____, therefore _____ will not fear. Lord, You are the stronghold of _____'s life and _____ will not be afraid!

> I have confidence in You Lord and I proclaim …

Psalm 30:2 – I called on You for help and You healed me.

> ² *O LORD my God, I cried to you for help, and you have healed me.*

Let's Pray & Proclaim: I _____ have confidence Lord through Your Scripture that when I cry out to You, You hear me and I _____ proclaim that You have healed me. You are my God.

Now try praying this scripture by proclaiming it over your family, your situation or the community around you.

A Prayer of Proclamation & Confidence for our family or situation: I _____ have confidence Lord through Your Scripture that when I cry out to You, You hear me and I _____ proclaim that You have healed _____. You are our God.

> We give life to others and to situations by declaring God's word over them!

> Our Lord is our Healer.
> The Lord sustains us.

Psalm 41: 2-3 – The Lord sustains him on his sick bed and restores him from his illness.

> ² *The Lord protects them and keeps them alive; they are called happy in the land. You do not give them up to the will of their enemies.*
> ³ *The Lord sustains them on their sickbed; in their illness you heal all their infirmities.*

Proclamation: Lord, You protect _____ and sustain _____ in sickness. Lord You heal all _____ infirmities.

DO YOU REALIZE THAT IT IS GOD'S NATURE TO FAVOR AND HONOR US!

> No good thing does the Lord withhold.

Psalm 84:11 – God bestows favor and honor; no good thing does He withhold.

> *¹¹ For the LORD God is a sun and shield; he bestows favor and honor. No good thing does the LORD withhold from those who walk uprightly.*

Proclamation: I _____ choose to walk upright. Guide me and aid me. As I do, I know, that You will withhold no good thing from me.

> **No evil shall befall me.**

Psalm 91:9-13 – The Lord is my refuge and dwelling place. On His hands He will bear me up.

> *⁹ Because you have made the LORD your refuge, the Most High your dwelling place, ¹⁰ no evil shall befall you, no scourge come near your tent. ¹¹ For he will command his angels concerning you to guard you in all your ways. ¹² On their hands they will bear you up, so that you will not dash your foot against a stone. ¹³ You will tread on the lion and the adder, the young lion and the serpent you will trample under foot.*

We are His!

Proclamation: Lord, I _____ choose to make You my refuge. I welcome You to dwell within me. Therefore, I _____ proclaim that no evil will befall me; that You will command Your angels concerning me and on Your hands You will bear me up.

> Notice the ownership in this Scripture.

Psalm 91:14-16 – Those who love me I will deliver, protect, answer, rescue, honor, etc.

> ¹⁴ *Those who love me, I will deliver; I will protect those who know my name.* ¹⁵ *When they call to me, I will answer them; I will be with them in trouble, I will rescue them and honor them.* ¹⁶ *With long life I will satisfy them, and show them my salvation.*

Proclamation: Lord, I _____ love You. I proclaim the promise You made that if I love You that You will deliver me, protect me, hear me when I call, answer my prayers, be with me in my troubles, rescue and honor me, and give me long life and salvation with You.

Proclamation over Others: Lord, _____ loves You. I proclaim the promise You made that if _____ loves You that You will deliver _____, protect them, hear them when they call, answer their prayers, be with them in their troubles, rescue and honor them, and give them long life and salvation with You.

You may have noticed by now that the scriptures on healing don't use words like:

> 'perhaps'
> 'maybe'
> 'sometimes'
> 'some people'
> and 'might work'

Nor do they use the phrase:

> 'once in a while'...

> Notice this recurring thought that He forgives *all* iniquity and He heals *all* diseases...

Psalm 103:2-5 — He forgives all your iniquity and heals all your diseases.

> *² Bless the LORD, O my soul, and do not forget all his benefits— ³ who forgives all your iniquity, who heals all your diseases, ⁴ who redeems your life from the Pit, who crowns you with steadfast love and mercy, ⁵ who satisfies you with good as long as you live so that your youth is renewed like the eagle's.*

Proclamation: I _____ bless You Lord, for You forgive all my iniquity and heal all my diseases. You Lord have redeemed me and crown me with Your steadfast love and mercy. You Lord will comfort me with good as long as I live, renewing me like the eagle's.

> God's Words Heal.

Psalm 107:19-21 – He sent forth his word and healed them.

> [19] Then they cried to the LORD in their trouble, and he saved them from their distress; [20] he sent out his word and healed them, and delivered them from destruction. [21] Let them thank the LORD for his steadfast love, for his wonderful works to humankind.

Proclamation: I _____ cried out to You Lord and You saved me from my distress. Lord, You sent out Your word and I am healed. Lord, You have delivered me from destruction. I thank You Lord for Your steadfast love and the wonderful works You do for me!

What conclusions are you drawing after reading and praying these scriptures?

_____

_____

**Let me tell you about the power of Proclamation...
When God's Word goes out it continues until it is complete .
Isaiah 55: 10-12.**

**In proclamation, we proclaim His Word over
our lives, our situation
our family,
in expectation
that it will do as it says.**

> These words are like a security blanket, that we can lay over situations!

Psalm 118:17 – I shall not die but I shall live and recount the deeds of the Lord!

> ¹⁷ I shall not die, but I shall live, and recount the deeds of the LORD.

Proclamation: I _____ shall not die, but I _____ shall live and recount the deeds of the Lord my God.

> He Heals!

Psalm 147:3 – He heals the brokenhearted.

> ³ He heals the broken hearted, and binds up their wounds.

Proclamation: I _____ am assured Lord, that it is in Your nature to heal my broken heart and bind my wounds.

Proclamation for Others: I _____ am assured Lord, that it is in Your nature to heal _____'s broken heart and bind _____'s wounds.

SECTION THREE:

SEEKING HIS PROMISES

> What do we keep in our attention, hearing, sight and heart? His Word.[3]

Proverbs 4:20-22 – Keep my Words in Your Attention, Hearing, Sight and Heart and they will give you Life and Health.

> ²⁰ *My child, be attentive to my words; incline your ear to my sayings.* ²¹ *Do not let them escape from your sight; keep them within your heart.* ²² *For they are life to those who find them, and healing to all their flesh.*

Let's Pray & Seek His Promise: Lord, each day I _____ keep Your Words in my Attention, Hearing, Sight and Heart and I hold fast to Your promise, that I will have Life and Healing to my whole body.

> Note the two-fold Promise for keeping His Word in our Attention, Hearing, Sight and Heart!

Proverbs 4:22 – There is a two-fold promise.

> ²² *For they are life to those who find them, and healing to all their flesh.*

Let's Pray & Seek His Promise: Lord, I _____ accept Your promise of Life and Health to my whole flesh.

There are a number of promises made to those who follow Jesus and keep His Commands including:

- **Life and health**
- **Peace**
- **Strength renewed**
- **No weapon formed against us will prosper.**

> What a promise – *Peace.*
> *YES!*

Isaiah 26:2-4 – The righteous who keep faith may enter the Gates where they will have peace.

> ² *Open the gates, so that the righteous nation that keeps faith may enter in.* ³ *Those of steadfast mind you keep in peace—in peace because they trust in you.* ⁴ *Trust in the LORD forever, for in the LORD GOD you have an everlasting rock.*

Let's Pray & Seek His Promise: Lord in faith each day I _____ open the Gates and enter into your steadfast peace. I _____ trust in You forever and Your Promise, You are my everlasting Rock.

> A Promise of strength renewed.

Isaiah 40:28-31 – Because I wait on the Lord my strength will be renewed.

> *²⁸ Have you not known? Have you not heard? The LORD is the everlasting God, the Creator of the ends of the earth. He does not faint or grow weary; his understanding is unsearchable. ²⁹ He gives power to the faint, and strengthens the powerless. ³⁰ Even youths will faint and be weary, and the young will fall exhausted; ³¹ but those who wait for the LORD shall renew their strength, they shall mount up with wings like eagles, they shall run and not be weary, they shall walk and not faint.*

Let's Pray & Seek His Promise: Our Father in heaven, Creator of Heaven and Earth, I _____ wait on You. I know and believe that those who wait on You shall be renewed, I will mount up with wings like eagles and I _____ shall run and not grow weary, I shall walk and not grow faint.

> The Lord Promises that *no weapon fashioned against us shall prosper.*

Isaiah 54:17 – No weapon fashioned against us shall prosper.

> *¹⁷ No weapon that is fashioned against you shall prosper, and you shall confute every tongue that rises against you in judgment. This is the heritage of the servants of the LORD and their vindication from me, says the LORD.*

Let's Pray & Seek His Promise: Lord I _____ accept Your authority; that no weapon fashioned against me will prosper and that I _____ will confute every tongue that rises against me in judgement.

> The Lord directs and empowers His children.

Matthew 10:7-8 – Directions to Proclaim, Cure, Raise, Cleanse and Cast Out.

> *⁷ As you go, proclaim the good news, 'The kingdom of heaven has come near.' ⁸ Cure the sick, raise the dead, cleanse the lepers, cast out demons. You received without payment; give without payment.*

Let's Pray & Seek His Promise: Lord I _____ accept Your authority; that You have told me _____ to go out into the World proclaim the good news and pray for the sick and they will be healed, to raise the dead, cleanse the lepers and cast out demons. I _____ will do as You say and accept the promise You made.

> God's Word goes forth and does not return void. *YES!*

Isaiah 55:10-11 – The Lord promises that His Word goes forth and does not return void.

> *[10] For as the rain and the snow come down from heaven, and do not return there until they have watered the earth, making it bring forth and sprout, giving seed to the sower and bread to the eater, [11] so shall my word be that goes out from my mouth; it shall not return to me empty, but it shall accomplish that which I purpose, and succeed in the thing for which I sent it.*

Let's Pray & Seek His Promise: Lord I _____ know that Your Word is true and that Your Word will go out and complete Your Divine purpose. I welcome Your will in my life 'done on earth as it is in heaven'.

> Make a point to do what it says and confess your sin and pray for healing.

James 5:16 – Confess and pray that you may be healed.

> **¹⁶ *Therefore confess your sins to one another, and pray for one another, so that you may be healed. The prayer of the righteous is powerful and effective.***

Let's Pray & Seek His Promise: I _____ am broken and I have sinned against You my God. I am not afraid to tell the world of my sin that I might receive Your Promise Lord. I confess to You Lord _____. Thank You for Your healing.

What are your conclusions after reading and praying these scriptures?

_____

_____

_____

SECTION FOUR:

PUTTING YOURSELF IN THE STORY

In Section Four we will be using our mind and imagination to ~~play~~ pray Scripture. Many times, in scripture the Lord used peoples' dreams and thoughts to help them through situations. In Matthew 13: 34 it states that Jesus always used parables and illustrations when he spoke. He encouraged people to see themselves in relationship to the story-line. Some of us when we hear these parables become the main character, some of us are observers and some of us stand in Jesus shoes.

Use your imagination to move through the Scripture verse. Enter in to each Scripture image and let you heart be free to experience the story: sounds, smells, visuals and feelings. As you experience the events, meditate on what they mean to you.

> It is a good story. Put yourself into the story. Which character in the story are you (Servant, Centurion or in the Crowd)?

Matthew 8:5-13 – Jesus heals the centurion's servant according to his faith.

> *⁵ When he entered Capernaum, a centurion came to him, appealing to him ⁶ and saying, "Lord, my servant is lying at home paralyzed, in terrible distress." ⁷ And he said to him, "I will come and cure him." ⁸ The centurion answered, "Lord, I am not worthy to have you come under my roof; but only*

speak the word, and my servant will be healed. ⁹ For I also am a man under authority, with soldiers under me; and I say to one, 'Go,' and he goes, and to another, 'Come,' and he comes, and to my slave, 'Do this,' and the slave does it." ¹⁰ When Jesus heard him, he was amazed and said to those who followed him, "Truly I tell you, in no one in Israel have I found such faith. ¹¹ I tell you, many will come from east and west and will eat with Abraham and Isaac and Jacob in the kingdom of heaven, ¹² while the heirs of the kingdom will be thrown into the outer darkness, where there will be weeping and gnashing of teeth."¹³ And to the centurion Jesus said, "Go; let it be done for you according to your faith." And the servant was healed in that hour.

I Imagine: Lord, the Centurion, a Roman Soldier, normally would order and not humble himself. I _____ like the Centurion, humble myself before You and ask for Your healing. Lord, I _____ know it does not matter what my position, nor how far I feel away from You, but only that I open to You.

- - -▶ **Spend some time in that image, watching what happens as you come humbly before the Lord and seek His Healing, Grace and Mercy.** ◀- - -

As we move from the Old Testament to the New Testament you will find that God is consistent, with what He says, in both Testaments.

> Did you know that in the Gospels only 2 people are commended as having 'great faith'?

Matthew 15: 21-28 – Jesus heals the daughter of the Canaanite Woman who has Great Faith.

²¹ Jesus left that place and went away to the district of Tyre and Sidon. ²² Just then a Canaanite woman from that region came out and started shouting, "Have mercy on me, Lord, Son of David; my daughter is tormented by a demon." ²³ But he did not answer her at all. And his disciples came and urged him, saying, "Send her away, for she keeps shouting after us." ²⁴ He answered, "I was sent only to the lost sheep of the house of Israel." ²⁵ But she came and knelt before him, saying, "Lord, help me." ²⁶ He answered, "It is not fair to take the children's food and throw it to the dogs." ²⁷ She said, "Yes, Lord, yet even the dogs eat the crumbs that fall from their masters' table." ²⁸ Then Jesus answered her, "Woman, great is your faith! Let it be done for you as you wish." And her daughter was healed instantly.

I Imagine: Jesus, the Canaanite Woman normally would or could not approach a Jewish man. I _____ like the woman with persistent faith, humble myself before You and ask for Your Healing. Lord, I _____ know it does not matter what my position nor how far I feel away from You, but only that I open to You.

The key in each of these Scriptures is openness.

We open to God's potential and He fulfills our dreams.

**Trust in the Lord with all your heart, acknowledge Him and He will take care of you.
Proverbs 3: 5 - 6**

> This is another good story. Put yourselves into the story. Which character in the story are you, (Peter, Peter's mom, Jesus, a person in the crowd, or the possessed?

Matthew 8:14-17 – Jesus heals Peter's mother.

> [14] When Jesus entered Peter's house, he saw his mother-in-law lying in bed with a fever; [15] he touched her hand, and the fever left her, and she got up and began to serve him. [16] That evening they brought to him many who were possessed with demons; and he cast out the spirits with a word, and cured all who were sick. [17] This was to fulfill what had been spoken through the prophet Isaiah, "He took our infirmities and bore our diseases."

I Imagine: Lord, like when You entered Peter's house You are welcome to enter my home today. Come touch and heal! Like You touched the many who were brought to You, come touch and heal today.

   "You took my infirmities and bore my diseases."

> Jesus heals the two blind men.
> Do you believe He can do it?
> Yes!

Matthew 9:27-30 – Jesus Heals Two Blind Men.

²⁷ As Jesus went on from there, two blind men followed him, crying loudly, "Have mercy on us, Son of David!" ²⁸ When he entered the house, the blind men came to him; and Jesus said to them, "Do you believe that I am able to do this?" They said to him, "Yes, Lord." ²⁹ Then he touched their eyes and said, "According to your faith let it be done to you." ³⁰ And their eyes were opened. Then Jesus sternly ordered them, "See that no one knows of this."

I Imagine: Lord, I _____ believe You can heal. Come and touch _____ with Your Healing Love. Renew and bless them!

> Jesus heals every disease and sickness!

Matthew 9:35 – Jesus went through the villages healing every disease & sickness.

> [35] Then Jesus went about all the cities and villages, teaching in their synagogues, and proclaiming the good news of the kingdom, and curing every disease and every sickness.

I Imagine: Lord, like the many You healed, I _____ need Your touch. Heal me today, Lord. You cure every disease and every sickness.

- - -▶ *Spend some time in that image, this village scene, watching what happens as you come humbly before the Lord and seek His Healing, Grace and Mercy.* ◀- - -

We use our imagination, all our senses, to reach out to Our God for His touch in our life.

> You are to put your faith in God's healing.

Mark 5:34 – Daughter your faith has healed you.

> *³⁴ He said to her, "Daughter, your faith has made you well; go in peace, and be healed of your disease."*

I Imagine: Lord, I _____ have Faith in You that You can make me well. Thank You for Your gift of Peace and Healing my disease.

> Lord, anything is possible,
> Help my unbelief!

Mark 9:20-25 – Possessed Boy - Help my unbelief.

> *²⁰ And they brought the boy to him [Jesus]. When the spirit saw him, immediately it convulsed the boy, and he fell on the ground and rolled about, foaming at the mouth. ²¹ Jesus asked the father, "How long has this been happening to him?" And he said, "From childhood. ²² It has often cast him into the fire and into the water, to destroy him; but if you are able to do anything, have pity on us and help us." ²³ Jesus said to him, "If you are able!—All things can be done for the one who believes." ²⁴ Immediately the father of the child cried out, "I believe; help my unbelief!" ²⁵ When Jesus saw that a crowd came running together, he rebuked the unclean spirit, saying to it, "You spirit that keeps this boy from speaking and hearing, I command you, come out of him, and never enter him again!"*

> *I Imagine: Lord, I _____ know that 'all things can be done for one who believes'. Lord, I _____ come into Your presence and place this request _____. You are the Creator and all things are possible in Your power.*

- - -▶ *Spend some time in that image, with the possessed boy, watching what happens as you come humbly before the Lord and seek His Healing, Grace and Mercy.* ◀- - -

**The Holy Spirit is poured out on all of us that we may Prophesy, Dream dreams and see Visions.
Joel 2: 28-29 / Acts 2: 17-18**

> Lord, You have the power to create and the power to destroy.

Mark 11:20-25 – The Lesson from the Withered Fig Tree.

[20] In the morning as they passed by, they saw the fig tree withered away to its roots. [21] Then Peter remembered and said to him, "Rabbi, look! The fig tree that you cursed has withered." [22] Jesus answered them, "Have faith in God. [23] Truly I tell you, if you say to this mountain, 'Be taken up and thrown into the sea,' and if you do not doubt in your heart, but believe that what you say will come to pass, it will be done for you. [24] So I tell you, whatever you ask for in prayer, believe that you have received it, and it will be yours. [25] "Whenever you stand praying, forgive, if you have anything against anyone; so that your Father in heaven may also forgive you your trespasses."

> *I Imagine: Lord, I ____ ask in Your Name and believe without doubt what Jesus has said, "whatever you ask for in prayer, believe that you have received it, and it will be yours". I now ask in faith _____ .*

- - -▶ *Matthew 11 asks us to do an inventory of those we need to forgive, in order that we may obtain the Lord's forgiveness. Enter the story again - think of forgiveness.* ◀- - -

We put our faith and trust in the Lord. He is our provider.

**²⁶ Look at the birds of the air;
they neither sow nor reap
nor gather into barns,
and yet your heavenly
Father feeds them.
Are you not of more
value than they?
Matthew 6:26**

> Faith is an element in healing. Faith is a Gift from God's Holy Spirit.

Luke 8:43-48 – Women who touched Jesus cloak is healed.

> *[43] Now there was a woman who had been suffering from hemorrhages for twelve years; and though she had spent all she had on physicians, no one could cure her. [44] She came up behind him and touched the fringe of his clothes, and immediately her hemorrhage stopped. [45] Then Jesus asked, "Who touched me?" When all denied it, Peter said, "Master, the crowds surround you and press in on you." [46] But Jesus said, "Someone touched me; for I noticed that power had gone out from me." [47] When the woman saw that she could not remain hidden, she came trembling; and falling down before him, she declared in the presence of all the people why she had touched him, and how she had been immediately healed. [48] He said to her, "Daughter, your faith has made you well; go in peace."*

These Scriptures emphasize our responsibility and our authority.

> I have authority in Christ Jesus!

Luke 10:19 – I, Jesus, have given you authority to tread over the enemy in all his forms.

> *¹⁹ See, I have given you authority to tread on snakes and scorpions, and over all the power of the enemy; and nothing will hurt you.*

I Imagine: Lord, I _____ stand ready as You're soldier to trample on snakes and scorpions and with You're power I _____ wield power over the enemy. Nothing will hurt me!

> Who is the thief?
> Who has conquered him?

John 10:10 – The thief came to destroy. Christ came to give us life!

> *¹⁰ The thief comes only to steal and kill and destroy [sickness is stealing, killing and destroying..] I came that they may have life [health..] and have it abundantly [to the full; till it overflows..]*

I Imagine: Lord, I _____ stand in Your Presence and Authority to fend off the attacks of the thief. I _____ receive Life, Health and Abundance from You. Let Your River flow!

- - -▶ One can enter the image again reflecting on the areas in our life or the lives of those around us where the thief is stealing, killing and destroying. Invite the Lord of life, to pour out His healing and abundance. ◀- - -

> Jesus tells us we will do even more than He…

John 14:12 – Jesus said I _____ will do even greater…

> *¹² Very truly, I tell you, the one who believes in me will also do the works that I do and, in fact, will do greater works than these, because I am going to the Father.*

I Imagine: Lord, I _____ believe in You and the many Miraculous Works You preformed. I _____ will walk in Your power and do Your work, beyond imagination!

What are your conclusions after reading and praying these scriptures?

_____

_____

_____

NOTES:

[1] Fabbi, Kenneth L., *Five Fold Cycle - Method of Healing Personal Hurt: Healing Life's Hurts,* Lethbridge, Alberta, Canada: Kenneth L. Fabbi, 2019.

[2] Roycroft, Thomas W. and Kenneth L. Fabbi. *You Can Minister Spiritual Gifts.* Lethbridge, Alberta, Canada: Kenneth L. Fabbi, 2019.

[3] This teaching is entitled *Scripture as Medicine.* It explains the two-fold Promise when we keeping God's Word in our Attention, Hearing, Sight and Heart. It was used with permission, from the vast resources of Fr. John Hampsch, CMF, Claretian Teaching Ministry, http://catholicbooks.net/

APPENDIX 1:

WHAT IS PRAYER

> What is Prayer?
> (a two way dialogue)
> — Body / Mind / Spirit in communication with God

PRAYER DEFINED IN THE BIBLE IS:

1. A lifting up our soul to God: Psalm 25:1; 143: 8
2. Trusting we pouring out our heart to God: Psalm 62: 8
3. A crying out to God: Psalm 86: 3
4. Telling Him your needs; 1 Peter 5: 7
5. It is turning from our sin and turning to God to cleanse us: Acts 3: 19
6. Spiritual incense to God: Revelations 5: 8
7. Coming before the Throne of Grace: Psalm 84: 1-2; Hebrews 4: 16
8. Listening with expectation: Psalm 5: 3; 17: 6
9. Prayer is a sacrifice of praise & the fruit of our lips: Hebrews 13: 15
10. Drawing close to God in friendship, fellowship and trust – it is a relationship: James 4: 8

www.ingramcontent.com/pod-product-compliance
Lightning Source LLC
Chambersburg PA
CBHW050447010526
44118CB00013B/1714